THE WHISTLE BLOWER WORKBOOK

THE MENTAL TOUGHNESS WORKBOOK FOR REFEREES, UMPIRES, AND SPORTS OFFICIALS

DR. JO LUKINS

Copyright © 2025 by Dr. Jo Lukins

All rights reserved.

No part of this book may be reproduced in any form or by any electronic or mechanical means, including information storage and retrieval systems, without written permission from the author, except for the use of brief quotations in a book review.

ISBN: 978-1-7635127-4-0 (Paperback)

Editor: Marinda Wilkinson

Elite Edge Publishing

www.drjolukins.com

THE MORE THAT YOU READ, THE MORE THINGS YOU WILL KNOW. THE MORE THAT YOU LEARN, THE MORE PLACES YOU'LL GO."

- DR SEUSS

A MESSAGE FROM DR. JO

My passion for reading and learning runs deep. Yet, I've noticed a consistent pattern for myself and others: turning insights into real action often requires more than simply understanding a good idea; it takes deliberate engagement. From both research and my own workshop experience, I've seen that people learn in distinct ways: some absorb information by listening, others by observing, and many through hands-on experiences. What about you? How do you best translate knowledge into action?

For me, meaningful change starts with writing. There's wisdom in the message: *When you write something down, you hear it twice*; once in your mind, then again as you write it on the page. Writing helps to clarify intention and solidify learning.

That's why I created this workbook to accompany The Whistle Blower. Rather than passively consuming each rule, you'll find dedicated worksheets aligned with every principle, designed for active reflection and real application. My suggestion: don't try to tackle everything at once. With 12 core rules, each with 3 practical subrules (plus a bonus), you have a toolkit of 37 actionable ideas. Begin by prioritizing the rules that resonate most with you or match your current challenges. There's great value in choosing your own path; focus on what will be most helpful for you right now.

True learning is a journey. Research, and my experience teaching skills shows that slow, intentional practice is what transforms ideas into lasting habits. Take your time. Deepen your understanding of each rule before moving ahead. To support this, I've included a checklist where you can record when you start and finish working on each lesson, a small structure to help you track progress and growth.

If questions arise as you work through the material, please email me. Your feedback not only helps improve these resources but also shapes what I share next.

Dr. Jo

THE WHISTLE BLOWER WORKBOOK CHECKLIST

This workbook does not need to be completed in order. Select the rules that are most relevant to you. Use these pages as a checklist for the rules you have worked on to keep track of your learning and progress.

- [ ] 1.1 Own Your Preparation—The Winning Edge
- [ ] 1.2 Inspect and Prepare—The Devil is in the Details
- [ ] 1.3 Visualize Success—Mind Over Matter
- [ ] 2.1 Sleep Like a Champion—Rest for Success
- [ ] 2.2 Peak Fitness for Peak Performance—The Physical Edge
- [ ] 2.3 Fuel Your Mind—Nutrition for Excellence
- [ ] 3.1 Arrive Early, Leave Later—The Time Advantage
- [ ] 3.2 Learn from the Past, Stay Present, Be Ready for the Future
- [ ] 3.3 Plan for Overtime Before It Happens—Anticipate and Adapt
- [ ] 4.1 Control What You Can, Accept What You Can't
- [ ] 4.2 Think Before You Act—Consequences of Each Call
- [ ] 4.3 Influence Through Presence—Your Body Speaks First
- [ ] 5.1 Trust Your Instincts—The Power of Decision Conviction
- [ ] 5.2 Mindful Presence—Being in the Moment
- [ ] 5.3 Focus and Process—The Art of Mental Filtering
- [ ] 6.1 Clear and Confident Communication
- [ ] 6.2 Non-Verbal Communication—The Unspoken Language
- [ ] 6.3 Adaptive Communication—Flexibility in Action
- [ ] 7.1 Positive Self-Talk—The Power of Helpful Thinking
- [ ] 7.2 Constructive Self-Reflection—Learning from Experience
- [ ] 7.3 Mental Reset Techniques—Regain Your Focus
- [ ] 8.1 Rapid Mental Rebound Technique—Quick Recovery
- [ ] 8.2 Building Mental Resilience—The Long Game
- [ ] 8.3 Mental Recovery During Breaks—Recharge and Refocus
- [ ] 9.1 Emotional Control—Staying Calm Under Fire
- [ ] 9.2 Composure Techniques—Keeping Your Cool

- 9.3 Pressure as Opportunity—Turning Stress into Strength
- 10.1 Systematic Self-Evaluation—The Path to Progress
- 10.2 Progress Tracking and Celebration—Measuring Success
- 10.3 Feedback and Sharing—Learning from Others
- 11.1 Building Relationships—The Power of Community
- 11.2 Mentorship and Learning—Passing on Wisdom
- 11.3 Community Support—Standing Together
- 12.1 Cultivating Curiosity—The Mind of a Learner
- 12.2 Practicing Gratitude—Finding Positivity
- 12.3 Continuous Learning and Growth
- Bonus rule: Holistic Well-being—Balancing Life and Sport

RULE 1
PRE-GAME PLAYBOOK

"One important key to success is self-confidence. An important key to self-confidence is preparation."
—*Arthur Ashe*

Rule 1.1: Own Your Preparation—The Winning Edge
Rule 1.2: Inspect and Prepare—The Devil is in the Details
Rule 1.3: Visualize Success—Mind Over Matter

This mental rule emphasizes the importance of a comprehensive pre-game routine. Mastering your preparation lays the foundation for confident and effective officiating, ensuring you step onto the field or court ready to handle the game's challenges.

RULE 1.1

OWN YOUR PREPARATION—THE WINNING EDGE

Create your match plan: Develop a checklist that works for you. Make it personal. This might include reviewing recent rule changes, checking your equipment, or doing light stretching. Your pre-game plan might look something like this:

24 hours before:
- ☐ Lock in game details (double-check time and location)
- ☐ Plan your travel (account for traffic and parking)
- ☐ Lay out your uniform and gear (inspect for any issues)
- ☐ Pack your bag (whistle, cards, watch, notebook)

Game day:
- ☐ Fuel up right (balanced meal 2-3 hours before game time)
- ☐ Hydrate consistently (start early and continue throughout the day)

The final countdown:
- ☐ Arrive early (aim for at least 30 minutes before starting)
- ☐ Warm up body and mind (light jog, stretch, and mental rehearsal)
- ☐ Meet with fellow officials (align on key points)

Create a pre-game checklist.

What are all the elements that help you arrive prepared and ready to go?

List them in as much detail as you need and then tick them as you complete them.

Set your targets.
Before each match, choose one or two key targets you want to focus on. For example, you might want to improve your field position or enhance your communication with assistant referees.

Aim to make your goals SMARTER:
Specific: Be clear about exactly what you want to achieve.
Measurable: Decide how you'll track your success.
Attainable: Choose goals that are within your reach for this game.
Realistic: Make sure your targets are practical, not overwhelming.
Time-Based: Set a timeframe - usually by the end of the match - to achieve your goal.
Evaluate: After the game, review how you did against your targets.
Revise: Adjust your goals for your next match based on what you've learned.

You'll see steady improvement in your officiating performance by setting, evaluating, and regularly adjusting your targets.

Know your "why".

Reflect on your personal "why" as an official: What motivates you? Whether it's a love for the game, a commitment to fairness, or the enjoyment of supporting athletes, describe what fuels your dedication.

How does keeping your motivation in mind help you stay focused and handle the challenges of officiating?

Pre-game inspection routine might look:
1. Arrive at the venue early, allowing ample time for a thorough inspection.
2. Take a deep breath and mentally transition into "referee mode" as you begin the process.
3. Conduct a purposeful walk around the entire playing area.
4. Check all court/field markings, ensuring they are clear and accurate.
5. Inspect goal posts, nets, baskets, or other sport-specific equipment.
6. Examine game balls, verifying proper inflation and condition.
7. If applicable, test any electronic equipment (e.g., communication devices, scoring systems).
8. Incorporate the inspection into a broader pre-match routine, including physical warm-up and mental preparation exercises.

By following these steps, referees can maximize the pre-game inspection routine's practical and psychological benefits. This structured approach helps reduce anxiety, enhance focus, and boost confidence, setting the stage for effective officiating performance.

Create a pre-game inspection routine.

What are all the elements that help you arrive prepared and ready to go?

List them in as much detail as you need and then tick them off as you complete them.

RULE 1.3
VISUALIZE SUCCESS—MIND OVER MATTER

Here's a step-by-step guide for your visualization script:

Step 1: Set a clear objective
    Decide on specific scenarios you want to visualize.

Step 2: Engage all your senses
    Ask yourself:
    What can you see? hear? touch? feel?
    - Sight: Picture the players, field, and surroundings
    - Sound: Imagine the crowd noise, whistle, and player talk
    - Touch: Feel the whistle in your hand or the motion of signaling
    - Emotion: Envision the calm confidence while making calls

Step 3: Visualize success
    Always imagine yourself performing at your best. See yourself:
    - Making confident, accurate calls
    - Staying composed during difficult interactions
    - Positioning yourself perfectly to follow the play

Step 4: Change perspectives
    Visualize from different viewpoints:
    - First-person perspective (what you would see)
    - Third-person perspective (how others would see you)

Step 5: Practice regularly

Dedicate 5-10 minutes to visualization before every game. Make it a routine to enhance your mental readiness gradually.

Step 6: Combine with physical practice

Reinforce your visualization by physically practicing the actions you've mentally rehearsed. For example, practice running the court or field in a real-life setting after visualizing your positioning.

Write out your visualization script in the space below (or in your journal). You may also find it helpful to record the script on your phone and listen to it prior to games. Would you like some feedback on it? Email it to me (excel@drjolukins.com), and I'll share my thoughts with you.

RULE 2

MIND AND BODY IN SYNC

*"Every decision starts with a clear mind and a prepared body.
That's how you stay sharp under pressure."*
—*Becky Sauerbrunn*

Rule 2.1: Sleep Like a Champion—Rest for Success
Rule 2.2: Peak Fitness for Peak Performance—The Physical Edge
Rule 2.3: Fuel Your Mind—Nutrition for Excellence

THIS NEXT RULE EMPHASIZES THE CRITICAL IMPORTANCE OF mind, rest, and fuel for performance. By prioritizing these factors, you lay the foundation to better handle whatever challenges officiating may present.

RULE 2.1

SLEEP LIKE A CHAMPION—REST FOR SUCCESS

Try this sleep performance challenge.
 1. Week one - Sleep log

Day	Bedtime	Waketime	Total sleep	Disruptions	Overall performance
Monday					
Tuesday					
Wednesday					
Thursday					
Friday					
Saturday					
Sunday					

Record bedtime, wake time, and total sleep hours. Note any disruptions falling asleep & rate your overall performance the following day (1-10). *It's important not to change your usual routine during this week

2. Week 2 – *Adapt your sleep routine with small changes*

Note changes to your bedtime routine here:

_____

_____

_____

_____

Track your sleep routine.

Day	Bedtime	Waketime	Total sleep	Disruptions	Overall performance
Monday					
Tuesday					
Wednesday					
Thursday					
Friday					
Saturday					
Sunday					

4. *Compare the two weeks:*
What are the improvements in sleep duration and quality?

_____

_____

_____

Are there changes in your performance ratings?

_____

_____

_____

What are the lessons from your sleep experiment? What changes do you want to have ongoing?

_____

_____

_____

RULE 2.2

PEAK FITNESS FOR PEAK PERFORMANCE— THE PHYSICAL EDGE

Physical training reflection questions to review. You may want to consult with an expert trainer for their professional advice in this area.

1. Am I consistently meeting my fitness goals for each training session?
2. How well am I recovering between matches and training sessions?
3. Are there any areas of physical fitness where I'm falling short of the demands of my matches?
4. How effectively am I balancing my physical training, officiating schedule, and other life commitments?
5. Am I incorporating enough variety in my workouts to prevent boredom and plateaus?
6. How does my current fitness level compare to the standards required for my level of officiating?
7. Are there any recurring injuries or physical issues that I need to address in my training?

8. Are there any new training techniques or technologies that could benefit my physical preparation?
9. How well am I tracking and measuring my progress in physical fitness?

Write your notes and reflections here:

RULE 2.3

FUEL YOUR MIND—NUTRITION FOR EXCELLENCE

Nutrition reflection questions to review. You may want to consult with a nutritionist or dietitian for their professional advice in this area.

1. Am I consistently fueling my body with balanced meals before and after matches?
2. How does my energy level fluctuate throughout a match, and could it be related to my nutrition?
3. Am I staying adequately hydrated before, during, and after officiating?
4. Do I notice any changes in my focus or decision-making abilities based on what I've eaten?
5. How well am I balancing my nutritional needs with my officiating schedule and lifestyle?
6. Are there any specific foods that affect my performance positively or negatively?
7. Am I consuming enough nutrients to support my recovery between matches and training sessions?

8. How does my current diet align with the nutritional recommendations for high-performance officials?
9. Should I consider incorporating any new nutritional strategies or supplements?
10. How well am I planning my meals to ensure optimal nutrition, especially on match days?

Write your notes and reflections here:

RULE 3

MASTER YOUR TIME

"Anticipate the future and adapt accordingly."
—*Wayne Gretzky*

Rule 3.1: Arrive Early, Leave Later—The Time Advantage
Rule 3.2: Learn from the Past, Stay in the Present, Be Ready for the Future—Timeless Wisdom
Rule 3.3: Plan for Overtime Before It Happens—Anticipate and Adapt

This rule is all about using time to your advantage. By learning from what's happened previously, staying focused on what's happening now, and being ready for what might happen next, you'll make better calls and handle games more smoothly. It's about being in the right headspace at the right time, from the pre-game preparations to the final whistle.

RULE 3.1

ARRIVE EARLY, LEAVE LATER—THE TIME ADVANTAGE

Map out your timing schedule to have yourself ready to go come game time. Add up the minutes to establish how much time you need to get ready.

Night before the game	
Day of the game	

RULE 3.2

LEARN FROM THE PAST, STAY IN THE PRESENT, BE READY FOR THE FUTURE— TIMELESS WISDOM

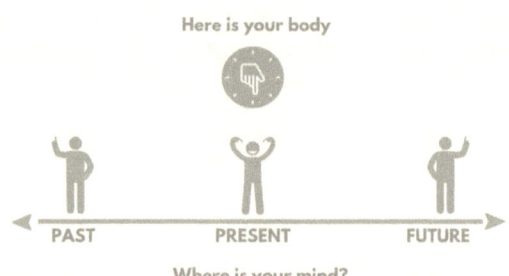

Keep your head in the *right* place at the *right* time

Referees often need assistance redirecting their thoughts from the past or future to the present. A simple yet effective three-step process can help:

1. *Take a breath*: Mental strategies are more effective when you're relaxed in the moment.

2. *Anchor yourself*: Focus on something in your immediate environment (use your senses – what can you see, hear or feel?)

3. *Redirect attention*: As you become aware of the present moment, consciously focus on the task.

The next time you get caught up thinking about what *has* happened or you're overthinking about what will happen, follow the process: take a breath | anchor yourself (senses) | redirect your attention.

The question, "What's important now?" can be helpful.

What are the thoughts (future or past) that take you out of focusing on the present?

What anchoring strategies will you use to bring you back to the now?

RULE 3.3

PLAN FOR OVERTIME BEFORE IT HAPPENS—ANTICIPATE AND ADAPT

To effectively plan for overtime, referees should:

1. *Study and internalize overtime rules*:

- ☐ Thoroughly review the specific overtime regulations for your sport and league.
- ☐ Understand any differences between regular season and playoff overtime procedure.
- ☐ Practice visualizing various overtime scenarios and your responses to them.

2. *Develop a mental checklist*:

- ☐ Create a brief mental list of key points to review before overtime begins.
- ☐ Include items such as timeouts remaining, player eligibility, and any specific overtime rules.

3. Establish clear communication protocols:
☐ Discuss overtime procedures with your officiating crew before the game.
☐ Agree on how you'll communicate important information during overtime.
☐ Plan how to convey overtime rules to team captains and coaches effectively.

4. Prepare physically and mentally:
☐ Incorporate endurance training into your routine to maintain stamina during extended play.
☐ Practice relaxation techniques to manage stress during high-pressure moments.
☐ Use visualization to rehearse successful overtime officiating mentally.

5. Review past experiences:
☐ Reflect on previous overtime situations you've officiated.
☐ Identify areas for improvement and successful strategies to replicate.
☐ Discuss overtime experiences with fellow officials to gain additional insights.

6. Stay updated on rule changes:
☐ Regularly check for any updates or modifications to overtime rules.
☐ Attend officiating clinics or workshops that cover overtime procedures.
☐ Participate in online forums or discussions about overtime officiating challenges.

A section for jotting down notes to help you get ready for overtime scenarios.

RULE 3.3   29

RULE 4

THE POWER OF THE WHISTLE

"You can't always control circumstances. However, you can always control your attitude, approach, and response."
—*Tony Dungy*

Rule 4.1: Control What You Can, Accept What You Can't—The Art of Letting Go
Rule 4.2: Think Before You Act—Consequences of Each Call
Rule 4.3: Influence Through Presence—Your Body Speaks First

EFFECTIVE OFFICIATING ISN'T ABOUT BEING THE LOUDEST OR using your whistle most frequently. It's about maintaining game flow through your presence alone. By mastering these principles, you'll enhance your control on the field, make better decisions under pressure, and maintain the game's integrity with confidence and authority.

RULE 4.1

CONTROL WHAT YOU CAN, ACCEPT WHAT YOU CAN'T—THE ART OF LETTING GO

Stephen Covey's *Circle of Influence Framework* categorizes factors into three concentric circles: the Circle of Control (inner), the Circle of Influence (middle), and the Circle of Concern (outer).

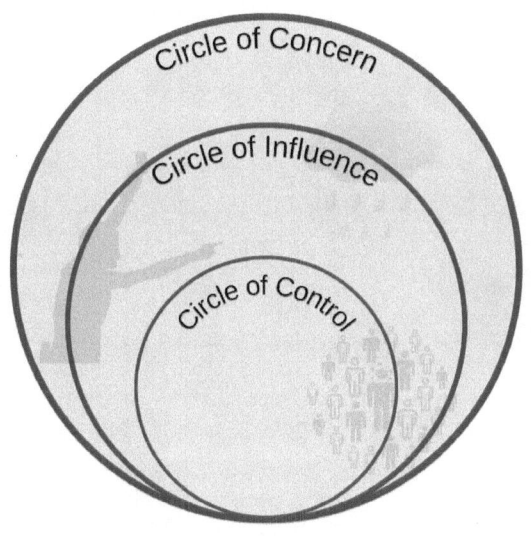

List Your Controllables: Write down everything you can control on game day (e.g., preparation, focus, decision-making, communication).

___

Identify Uncontrollables: Make a list of things you cannot control (like weather, team reactions, or crowd behavior). Reflect on how you currently respond to these and how you might let go more easily.

___

Map your controllables and uncontrollables onto Covey's Circles of Influence.

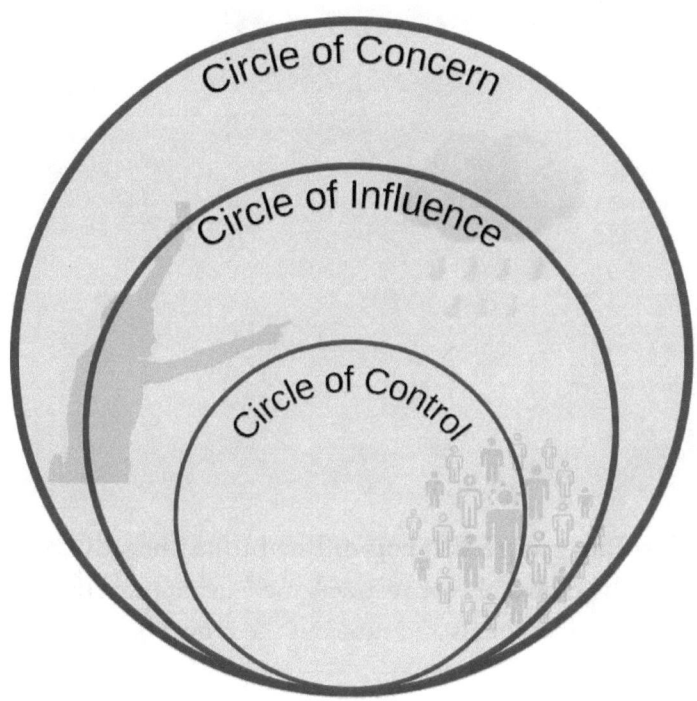

Action Planning: For each controllable factor, set one or two concrete actions you'll take to improve (e.g., "I will spend 10 minutes visualizing positive decisions before each game").

_____
_____
_____
_____

Proactive Language Exercise: Rewrite any negative or reactive thoughts ("The crowd always distracts me") using proactive language ("I will focus on my signals and tune out the crowd").

_____
_____
_____
_____

Routine Self-Review: Schedule regular check-ins after games where you evaluate your focus on your Circle of Influence, noting what worked and what you want to improve for next time.

Reflection Prompt: After each match, journal about one situation you handled well by focusing on your influence, and one scenario where you could shift attention away from uncontrollables next time.

Implement in-game strategies: During the game, use techniques to maintain focus on controllable elements:
- Use a trigger word or physical gesture to reset your focus when distracted by the uncontrollable.
- Practice mindfulness techniques to stay present and aware of your immediate surroundings.
- Develop a consistent decision-making process to rely on in high-pressure moments.

Utilize natural breaks: Use timeouts, quarter breaks, or other natural pauses in play to reassess and refocus on your circles of control and influence. This might involve:
- A quick body scan to check for tension and release it.
- A brief mental review of your performance so far, focusing on areas you can improve.
- Setting a specific intention for the next period of play.

RULE 4.2

THINK BEFORE YOU ACT—CONSEQUENCES OF EACH CALL

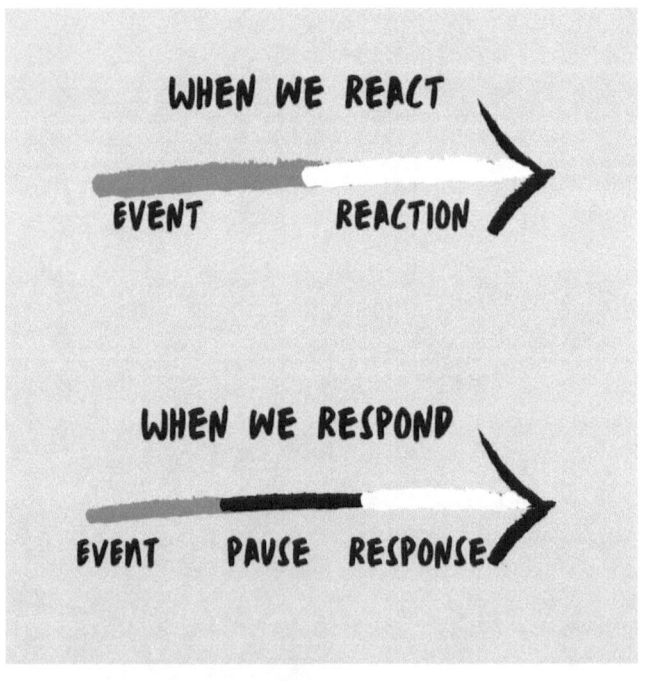

Scenario Reflection

Read the three scenarios below. For each, write down:

What might your immediate reaction be?

What could your considered response look like after taking a pause?

Scenario 1:

A player aggressively argues with you after you make a call.

Scenario 2:

You feel the crowd begin to boo loudly after a controversial decision.

Scenario 3:
You realize you made a mistake in your last call.

_____

_____

_____

_____

_____

Pause Techniques
List **two pause techniques** you could use in these situations (e.g., taking a deep breath, brief self-talk, stepping back).

_____

_____

_____

_____

Personal Application

Think about a time outside of refereeing (at work, home, or in another activity) where you reacted quickly to a stressful event.

Briefly describe what happened.

Looking back, how could a pause have helped you respond differently?

Reflection:

Which pause technique do you think will be most helpful for you in your future officiating? Why?

RULE 4.3

INFLUENCE THROUGH PRESENCE—YOUR BODY SPEAKS FIRST

Practice the techniques on the following pages to work on communicating through your body language. Use the space provided to jot down your reflections and insights about your thoughts and experiences.

Power Pose Practice

- Stand tall, feet shoulder-width apart.
- Raise your arms in a "V" above your head.
- Hold this position for 2 minutes while breathing slowly and deeply.
- As you hold the pose, silently repeat to yourself: "I am confident and in control."
- Afterwards, rate how confident and calm you feel on a scale of 1–10.

Tip: If possible, try this daily for a week and note any changes in your feelings before matches.

RULE 4.3

Triangle of Presence Drill

Stand in a ready position on the field or in front of a mirror, and mentally check:
Base: Are your feet stable and shoulder-width apart?
Core: Is your core engaged, posture upright?
Crown: Can you imagine a string gently pulling your head to the sky?

Practice moving several steps in different directions while maintaining this alignment.

After 5–10 repetitions, write a quick note: "What feels different about my balance and awareness?"

3-Point Presence Self-Check

During natural breaks in your next game (e.g., throw-in, timeout, at halftime):

Ask yourself:
Physical: Am I positioned to see both the action and reactions?
Mental: Does my body language show authority?
Spatial: Am I controlling my space or being influenced by others?

Record 1–2 observations after the game on your body positioning.

Mapping Presence Zones

Draw a simple map of your field or court. Mark and color three zones:
High Presence - conflict areas
Moderate Presence - near play but not directly involved
Observational Zone - away from main action
Note where you spent the most time.

																																				

Answer: "How might moving purposefully between these zones help you conserve your energy and stay effective?"

_____

_____

_____

Presence Anchors

Choose or create at least one anchor you'll use in the next match (e.g., a specific breathing pattern, gesture, or affirmation).

Describe your anchor:
What is it?
When will you use it?
After the next game, reflect: "Did my anchor help me boost my presence? Why or why not?"

_____

_____

_____

_____

_____

_____

_____

_____

_____

Body Language Awareness

Review a short video clip or photo of yourself officiating, or ask a colleague for feedback on your body language.

Write down:

What message do I think my body language sends to players and coaches?

One thing I will consciously adjust in my next game.

Reflection:

Which technique was most useful in helping you feel and project greater confidence and presence? How might consistent use of these techniques affect the way players, coaches, and spectators respond to you?

_____

_____

_____

_____

_____

_____

RULE 5

SPLIT-SECOND CLARITY

"The difference between something good and something great is attention to detail."
—*Charles R. Swindoll*

Rule 5.1: Trust Your Instincts—The Power of Decision Conviction
Rule 5.2: Mindful Presence—Being in the Moment
Rule 5.3: Focus

THIS MENTAL RULE EMPHASIZES THE IMPORTANCE OF CLARITY and quick decision-making in officiating. By trusting your instincts, staying mindfully present, and mastering the art of mental filtering, you'll be better equipped to make split-second decisions that keep the game flowing smoothly. In the dynamic environment of sports officiating, clarity of thought and action can make all the difference.

RULE 5.1

TRUST YOUR INSTINCTS—THE POWER OF DECISION CONVICTION

Practice the techniques on the following pages to work on strong decision making. Use the space provided to jot down your reflections and insights about your thoughts and experiences.

Pre-match mental rehearsal: Before each game, spend 5-10 minutes visualizing yourself making confident, quick decisions in various game scenarios. Find a quiet space and close your eyes. Imagine yourself on the field or court, facing different situations that require split-second decisions.

For example, visualize:
- A potential handball in soccer
- A close line call in tennis
- A charge/block situation in basketball

See yourself making these calls confidently and decisively. Feel the certainty in your body as you signal the decision. This mental practice primes your brain for decisive action during the actual game. More information on visualization can be found in Rule 1.3.

RULE 5.1   51

Pattern recognition training: Regularly review game footage to identify common patterns in play. Focus on recognizing meaningful cues that allow you to anticipate and respond effectively to game situations.

Set aside time each week to watch recordings of games in your sport. Pay attention to:
- How plays develop
- Player movements that often lead to fouls or violations
- Common scenarios that require quick decisions

As you watch, pause the video before the referee makes a call. Make your own decision, then compare it to the actual call. This practice will sharpen your ability to read the game and make quick, accurate decisions.

Post-game reflection: After each match, briefly review your key decisions. Note what went well and areas for improvement, focusing on the process rather than just the outcome.

Create a simple journal or use a notes app on your phone. After each game, spend 5-10 minutes answering these questions:

1. What were the 3-5 most crucial decisions I made today? For each decision:
2. Did I trust my initial instinct?
3. Was I able to make the call within 3 seconds?
4. How did my decision impact the game?
5. What patterns or situations do I need to study more?

This reflection helps reinforce good habits and identifies areas where you can improve your decision-making process.

Implementing the Quick Decision Toolkit

A gradual introduction of these rules will help you build your skills in making quick and effective decisions.

Week 1-2: Focus on the pre-match mental rehearsal. Make this a consistent part of your pre-game routine.

Week 3-4: Begin your pattern recognition training. Watch at least one game recording per week, focusing on decision-making moments.

Week 5-6: Start your post-game reflection practice. Keep it brief but consistent after each game.

By the end of six weeks, you should have a solid foundation in all three elements of the toolkit. Continue to practice and refine these skills throughout your officiating career.

UNTITLED 55

RULE 5.2

MINDFUL PRESENCE—BEING IN THE MOMENT

Practice the techniques on the following pages to work on being mindful in the moment. Use the space provided to jot down your reflections and insights about your thoughts and experiences.

Develop a pre-game centering routine: Create a short ritual to help you enter a state of mindful presence before each game. This might involve a series of deep breaths, a brief meditation, or a set of focusing exercises. The goal is to clear your mind of distractions. Practice this routine consistently so it becomes a natural part of your pre-game preparation. Write some notes here on what will be your focus.

Practice the three-breath reset: During natural breaks in play or moments of potential stress, use a quick breathing technique to re-center yourself. Take three slow, deep breaths, focusing your attention fully on each inhale and exhale. This simple practice can help you regain focus and composure in challenging situations. Make this reset a habit, using it regularly throughout the game to maintain your mindful presence.

Use physical anchors: Choose specific sensory cues to serve as reminders to stay present. This could be the feel of your whistle in your hand, the sound of your shoes on the court, or the sight of a particular part of the field or arena. Whenever you notice these anchors, use them as triggers to bring your attention back to the present moment. Regularly check in with these anchors throughout the game to maintain your mindful presence.

Engage in post-game reflection: After each game, take time to reflect on your level of mindful presence. Identify moments when you felt fully engaged and present, as well as times when your focus may have wavered. Consider what factors contributed to your state of mind in these situations. Use these insights to refine your approach and set specific goals for maintaining a mindful presence in future games.

RULE 5.3

FOCUS AND PROCESS—THE ART OF MENTAL FILTERING

Try the techniques on the following pages to work on mental filtering and blocking. Use the space provided to jot down your reflections and insights about your thoughts and experiences.

Force field visualization: Imagine an invisible force field around yourself that deflects distractions. When you perceive a distraction, visualize it hitting your force field and bouncing off, ensuring it doesn't affect your focus. This technique helps maintain a clear mental space, allowing you to focus on key game elements.

_____

_____

_____

Mindfulness and present moment focus: Practice mindfulness to stay fully engaged in the current moment. This involves focusing on each play as it happens without letting past mistakes or future worries cloud your judgment. Mindfulness helps you maintain composure and avoid overthinking, allowing you to make clear, objective decisions. By staying present, you can better recognize key cues in the game, such as player positions or rule violations, and respond accordingly.

Try the techniques on the following pages to work on mentally managing criticism. Use the space provided to jot down your reflections and insights about your thoughts and experiences.

Maintaining composure: It's helpful to remain calm and composed when faced with criticism. Rudeness says far more about the person criticizing than it does about you, so as best you can, avoid taking verbal abuse personally. Experienced referees emphasize the importance of not letting criticism affect their decisions, focusing instead on enforcing the rules impartially.

Thick skin and resilience: Developing a thick skin is crucial for handling criticism without letting it impact performance. Referees should remind themselves that personal attacks are commonplace and that their role is to make fair and unbiased decisions. Resilience grows with experience. It is helpful to adopt one of my favorite phrases, "we teach people how to treat us."

Constructive feedback: While negative feedback can be challenging, constructive feedback is essential for growth. Referees should seek feedback that focuses on improving their skills rather than personal attacks. This approach helps build confidence and enhances performance over time.

RULE 6
COMMAND, CONNECT, AND FOCUS

"Communication is not about speaking what we think. Communication is about ensuring others hear what we mean."
—*Simon Sinek*

Rule 6.1: Clear and Confident Communication—The Voice of Authority
Rule 6.2: Non-Verbal Communication—The Unspoken Language
Rule 6.3: Adaptive Communication—Flexibility in Action

THIS MENTAL RULE EMPHASIZES THE POWER OF EFFECTIVE communication in officiating. By mastering various communication techniques, you enhance your ability to command respect, connect with game participants, and maintain focus, ensuring smoother game management and increased credibility as an official. In officiating, how you communicate can be just as important as the decisions you make. Your words, actions, and presence all contribute to your effectiveness on the field or court.

RULE 6.1

CLEAR AND CONFIDENT COMMUNICATION— THE VOICE OF AUTHORITY

Practice the techniques on the following pages to work on clear and confident communication. Use the space provided to jot down your reflections and insights about your thoughts and experiences.

Develop your officiating voice: Your "officiating voice" should be distinct from your everyday speaking voice. It should be clear, authoritative, and projecting without shouting.

- Practice projecting your voice from your diaphragm, not your throat. This allows you to speak loudly without straining your voice.
- Work on enunciating clearly, especially when making calls or giving explanations.
- Record yourself making calls and listen to how you sound. Pay attention to clarity, tone, and confidence.

Master the three C's—Clear, Concise, Confident: Every verbal interaction should embody these three qualities.
Clear: Use simple, unambiguous language and avoid jargon
Concise: Get to the point quickly. In most situations, less is more.
Confident: Speak with authority, even if you're not feeling 100% sure.

   Practice crafting responses to common scenarios that embody these three C's. For example, "saying Out of bounds, red ball" instead of "I think it might have gone out off the blue player."

The explanation framework: Develop a mental framework for when and how to explain decisions when asked respectfully by a player or coach, to prevent misunderstandings that could escalate, to educate on lesser-known rules.
- State the outcome
- Cite the relevant rule
- Describe what you saw (briefly)
- Restate the outcome

An example could be, "The runner is out. A runner is out when he runs more than three feet away from his baseline to avoid being tagged. I saw the runner veer outside the baseline as the fielder attempted to apply the tag. Therefore, the runner is out."

The power of silence: Recognize that sometimes, the most powerful communication is no communication at all.
- After making a call, resist the urge to over-explain unless asked
- When faced with emotional reactions, allow a brief moment of silence before responding
- Use strategic pauses in your speech to emphasize important points

Practice incorporating deliberate silences into your communication during training or lower-stakes games.

Active listening techniques: Effective communication is a two-way street. Enhance your listening skills to improve overall communication.
- Practice maintaining eye contact when someone is speaking to you.
- Use non-verbal cues (like nodding) to show you're listening.
- Resist the urge to interrupt or formulate your response while others are speaking.

Post-game analysis: After each game, reflect on your communication:
- Identify moments where your communication was particularly effective or ineffective.
- Note any situations where you wish you had communicated differently.
- Seek feedback from colleagues or mentors specifically about your communication style.

Continuous improvement: Make clear and confident communication a focus of your ongoing development.
- Attend communication workshops or public speaking classes to refine your skills.
- Study videos of elite officials, paying attention to how they communicate in various situations.
- Practice your officiating voice and calls regularly, even outside of games.

RULE 6.2

NONVERBAL COMMUNICATION—THE UNSPOKEN LANGUAGE

Practice the techniques on the following pages to work on nonverbal communication. Use the space provided to jot down your reflections and insights about your thoughts and experiences.

Body language mastery: Develop a repertoire of non-verbal cues that project authority and control.
- Practice the "power pose": Stand tall with your feet shoulder-width apart, shoulders back, and chin up. Hold this pose for two minutes before games to boost confidence.
- Master the "neutral face": Develop a default expression that is alert and attentive but not emotional. Practice this in a mirror until it feels natural.
- Use deliberate hand gestures: Ensure your signals are crisp, clear, and decisive.
Practice these regularly to make them second nature.

The active listening triad: Implement these three components of active listening:
- Eye contact: Maintain appropriate eye contact when interacting with players or coaches. This shows engagement and commands respect.
- Body orientation: Turn your body towards the speaker, showing that you give them your full attention.
- Responsive nodding: Use subtle nods to acknowledge that you're listening, without necessarily agreeing.

The nonverbal toolkit: Develop a set of nonverbal tools for common officiating scenarios:

- The "calm down" gesture: A subtle, palms-down motion to de-escalate tensions without stopping play.
- The "I'm watching" look: A focused gaze that lets players know you're aware of developing situations.
- The "proximity control" technique: This involves moving closer to potential trouble spots without directly engaging, using your presence to maintain order.

Practice these in training sessions and gradually implement them in games.

Situational body language: Adapt your nonverbal cues to different game situations:
- High-tension moments: Project calm through slow, deliberate movements and controlled breathing.
- Routine calls: Use confident, assertive gestures to reinforce your decisions.
- Explanatory situations: Adopt an open, receptive posture when clarifying calls to players or coaches.

Role-play these situations with colleagues to refine your approach.

Cultural awareness: Recognize that nonverbal cues can have different meanings in different cultures.
- Research common nonverbal differences in cultures relevant to your officiating context.
- Be mindful of potentially offensive gestures and adapt your nonverbal toolkit accordingly.
- When officiating in unfamiliar cultural contexts, observe and mimic the nonverbal styles of respected local officials.

Self-management through nonverbals: Use nonverbal techniques to manage your own stress and project calm.
- Develop a subtle "reset" gesture when you feel tension rising.
- Practice deep, controlled breathing that's not visible to others but helps maintain your composure.
- Use power poses during breaks to recharge your confidence.

RULE 6.3

ADAPTIVE COMMUNICATION—FLEXIBILITY IN ACTION

Practice the techniques on the following pages to work on adaptive communication. Jot down your reflections in the space below.

Implement the temperature check technique: Regularly assess the emotional climate of the game to inform your communication approach. Develop a mental "temperature scale" from 1 (very calm) to 10 (extremely tense). Perform quick assessments at natural breaks in play and adjust your communication style based on the current "temperature." This will help you stay in tune with the game's emotional state and respond appropriately.

Maintain a feedback loop: Continuously refine your adaptive communication skills through feedback and reflection. After each game, reflect on key communication moments and their effectiveness. Seek input from colleagues or mentors about your communication style. Use this feedback to adjust and expand your adaptive strategies. This ongoing process of reflection and improvement will help you continually enhance your adaptive communication skills.

RULE 7
DISCOVER YOUR INNER COACH

"When I am right, no one remembers. When I am wrong, no one forgets."
—***Doug Harvey***

Rule 7.1: Positive Self-Talk—The Power of Helpful Thinking
Rule 7.2: Constructive Self-Reflection—Learning from Experience
Rule 7.3: Mental Reset Techniques—Regain Your Focus

This mental rule emphasizes the transformative power of inner dialogue. You can create a strong internal foundation that supports your officiating performance and resilience by mastering positive self-talk, constructive self-reflection, and mental reset techniques. Your inner voice is always with you—make it a coach who inspires confidence, growth, and excellence.

RULE 7.1

POSITIVE SELF-TALK—THE POWER OF HELPFUL THINKING

Practice the techniques on the following pages to work on helpful self talk. Use the space provided to jot down your reflections and insights about your thoughts and experiences.

Identify and challenge negative thoughts: Start by becoming aware of your inner dialogue, especially during challenging moments. When you notice unhelpful thoughts, challenge them with evidence-based positive alternatives. For example, if you think, "I always struggle with this type of call," reframe it to, "I've handled similar situations successfully before, and I'm well-prepared for this."

Develop a positive affirmation toolkit: Create a set of positive affirmations tailored to different officiating scenarios. These might include:

"I am well-prepared and confident in my abilities."

"I trust my judgment and make decisions with clarity."

"I remain calm and focused, even under pressure."

Practice these affirmations regularly during games and daily life to make them a natural part of your inner dialogue.

Use the "I will" technique: Replace phrases like "I can't" or "I hope" with "I will." This simple shift can significantly impact your mindset and approach to challenges. For instance, instead of thinking, "I hope I don't mess up this call," affirm, "I will make this call accurately and confidently."

Implement a pre-game mental routine: Develop a short pre-game ritual that includes positive self-talk. This may involve repeating your key affirmations, visualizing successful officiating scenarios, or taking a few deep breaths while reminding yourself of your capabilities. This routine can help set a positive tone for your inner dialogue throughout the game.

Practice self-compassion: Treat yourself with the same kindness and understanding you would offer a colleague or friend. When you make a mistake, acknowledge it without harsh self-criticism. Instead, use supportive language like, "I'm learning from this and will do better next time."

Use trigger words or phrases: Identify short, powerful words or phrases that can quickly reset your mindset during a game. These might be words like "focus," "confident," or "present." Use these triggers whenever you need a quick mental boost or refocus.

Conduct post-game positive reviews: After each game, take time to reflect on what went well. Identify specific moments where you demonstrated skill, composure, or good judgment. This practice reinforces positive self-talk and builds confidence for future games.

RULE 7.2

CONSTRUCTIVE SELF-REFLECTION— LEARNING FROM EXPERIENCE

Use the "what, so what, now what" framework to deepen your analysis of specific incidents or decisions. This approach helps you move from objective observation to meaningful analysis and actionable planning. It's a powerful tool for extracting valuable lessons from each officiating experience. Here is an example:

WHAT: *A player disputes a call, claiming it was incorrect.*
SO WHAT: The dispute affects the game's momentum and player morale. It also tests my ability to manage conflict.
NOW WHAT: I will review the play to ensure accuracy and communicate clearly with the player to resolve the issue.

Think back to a specific moment in your officiating—big or small—that left an impression on you (for example: a disputed call, missed play, or challenging interaction).

Work Through the Framework
For your chosen incident, answer the following in the space provided:
WHAT happened? Describe the incident objectively and concisely. Stick to the facts: *What did you observe? Who was involved? What actions were taken?*

_____

_____

_____

SO WHAT?
Analyze why the incident matters. *How did it affect the flow of the game, the participants, or your mindset? What challenges or issues did it highlight for you as an official?*

_____

_____

_____

NOW WHAT?

Decide on your future actions. *What will you do differently next time? Is there something you need to review, practice, or discuss with others? How will you apply what you learned the next time a similar situation arises?*

_____

_____

_____

Try to use the "What, So What, Now What" approach regularly after games or significant moments to strengthen your self-awareness and continuous improvement as an official.

WHAT?	
SO WHAT?	
NOW WHAT?	

WHAT?	
SO WHAT?	
NOW WHAT?	

WHAT?	
SO WHAT?	
NOW WHAT?	

WHAT?	
SO WHAT?	
NOW WHAT?	

WHAT?	
SO WHAT?	
NOW WHAT?	

WHAT?	
SO WHAT?	
NOW WHAT?	

RULE 7.3

MENTAL RESET TECHNIQUES—REGAIN YOUR FOCUS

Practice the techniques on the following pages to work on creating a mental reset. Use the space provided to jot down your reflections and insights about your thoughts and experiences.

Develop a quick reset ritual. You can use this strategy between plays or during natural breaks in the game. This might involve a specific breathing pattern, a physical gesture like adjusting your whistle, or a brief visualization of a calm, focused state. Practice this ritual regularly so it becomes second nature, allowing you to trigger a mental reset quickly and efficiently when needed.

Incorporate positive self-talk into your reset routine. Develop a set of short, empowering phrases that you can use to refocus your mind. These might include affirmations like "Next play," "Fresh start," or "Stay present." One of my favorites is W.I.N.—What's Important Now? This is a great phrase for helping you to orient your thinking to the present. Use these phrases consistently to reinforce a positive, forward-looking mindset.

Develop a strategy for handling particularly challenging or controversial moments. This might involve a slightly longer reset process, using the break between plays to take a few deep breaths, mentally reaffirming your expertise, and consciously letting go of any lingering emotions or doubts.

RULE 8
THE BOUNCE-BACK BLUEPRINT

"Toughness isn't just physical; it's the whisper of persistence when all odds stand against you."
—*Sandjest*

Rule 8.1: Rapid Mental Rebound Technique—Quick Recovery
Rule 8.2: Building Mental Resilience—The Long Game
Rule 8.3: Mental Recovery During Breaks—Recharge and Refocus

THIS MENTAL RULE EMPHASIZES THE POWER OF RESILIENCE IN officiating. Mastering recovery mechanisms enhances your ability to maintain consistent performance throughout the game, ensuring that individual setbacks don't derail one's overall effectiveness as an official. Resilience is not about avoiding falls, but mastering the art of rising. This rule equips you with the tools to rise stronger after every challenge, transforming potential setbacks into opportunities for growth and improved performance.

RULE 8.1

RAPID MENTAL REBOUND TECHNIQUE— QUICK RECOVERY

Practice the techniques on the following pages to work on quick recovery strategies. Use the space provided to jot down your reflections and insights about your thoughts and experiences.

Develop a consistent mental reset technique. This might involve taking a few deep breaths, visualizing a successful call, or using a specific phrase to refocus your attention. You can draw on some of the techniques you considered in rule 7.3. Practice this technique regularly so it becomes automatic, allowing you to clear your mind and move forward quickly.

_____

_____

_____

Create mental distance from difficult moments. This involves recognizing that mistakes are part of the game and not letting them define your performance. Practice self-compassion by acknowledging the error without dwelling on it. Instead, focus on what you can learn from the situation to improve.

Natural breaks in the game to reset quickly. During timeouts or between quarters, take a moment to reflect on your performance, identify areas for improvement, and mentally prepare for the next segment of the game. This proactive approach helps you maintain focus and composure, even when facing challenges.

RULE 8.2

BUILDING MENTAL RESILIENCE— THE LONG GAME

Practice the techniques on the following pages to work on mental resilience and overcoming setbacks. Use the space provided to jot down your reflections and insights about your thoughts and experiences.

Develop a challenge log. After each game, record one or two significant challenges you faced. For each challenge, write down:

- What happened
- How you responded
- What you learned
- How you'll apply this lesson in future games

This practice helps reframe difficulties as learning opportunities and builds a record of your growth over time.

Implement the perspective shift technique. When faced with a setback, ask yourself three questions:

- How important will this seem in a week? A month? A year?
- What can I learn from this situation?
- How can this experience make me a better official?

    This approach helps maintain a broader perspective and turns setbacks into opportunities for improvement.

Incorporate regular mental toughness training into your preparation routine. This could involve:
- Visualizing yourself handling difficult situations calmly and effectively.
- Practicing deep breathing or other relaxation techniques to use during games.
- Setting small, achievable challenges for yourself in each game (e.g., maintaining perfect positioning for an entire quarter).

Develop a quick reset ritual to practice self-forgiveness and maintain perspective under fire. This could be as simple as taking a deep breath, adjusting your cap or whistle, and mentally saying, "Next play." Use this ritual whenever you must let go of a mistake or refocus after a challenging interaction.

RULE 8.3

MENTAL RECOVERY DURING BREAKS—RECHARGE AND REFOCUS

To master the effective use of breaks and enhance your officiating performance, focus on implementing a structured approach to these crucial moments.

Develop a break routine. You can use a break routine consistently during time-outs, quarter breaks, or other pauses in play. This routine should include these key elements:

- *Mental reset*: Take three deep breaths, focusing on exhaling fully. As you breathe, visualize releasing any tension or residual emotions from the previous play or game segment.
- *Refocus*: Quickly review your key officiating priorities. Remind yourself of your positioning responsibilities and any specific aspects of the game you need to watch closely.
- *Perspective check*: Take a moment to consider the broader context of the game. Ask yourself: "What's the score? How much time is left? Are there any brewing tensions I need to be aware of?"
- Smile! You referee because it is a challenge for you and an enjoyable role. Smiling resets your emotional tone and makes relaxing and flowing through the game easier.

Practice this routine until it becomes second nature. This will allow you to complete these steps quickly and effectively, even during short breaks.

The emotional anchor technique for rapid emotional recovery. Choose a physical object you carry during games—perhaps your whistle or a small item in your pocket. When you feel emotions running high, touch this object and use it as a trigger to remind yourself to stay calm and objective. Over time, this physical action can become a powerful tool for quick emotional resets.

The zooming out habit during longer breaks. Mentally step back and consider the game as a whole to maintain a broader perspective:
- How has the overall tone of the game evolved?
- Are there any patterns in player behavior or team tactics you need to be aware of?
- How can you best contribute to a fair and well-managed conclusion to the contest?

This broader view can help you make more informed decisions and manage the game more effectively.

RULE 9
PRESSURE POINTS

"Pressure is a privilege."
—Virgil van Dijk

Rule 9.1: Emotional Control—Staying Calm Under Fire
Rule 9.2: Composure Techniques—Keeping Your Cool
Rule 9.3: Pressure as Opportunity—Turning Stress into Strength

THIS MENTAL RULE EMPHASIZES THE POWER OF EMBRACING pressure in officiating. By mastering pressure management techniques, you can perform at your best when it matters most, ensuring consistent, high-quality officiating even in the most challenging and high-stakes environments. Pressure doesn't break you; it reveals your true strength.

RULE 9.1
EMOTIONAL CONTROL—STAYING CALM UNDER FIRE

Practice the techniques on the following pages to work on strong emotional control. Use the space provided to jot down your reflections and insights about your thoughts and experiences.

Develop an emotional anchor. This is a quick, discreet action you can perform to center yourself in heated moments. It might be taking a deep breath, touching your whistle, or briefly closing your eyes. Practice using this anchor regularly, even in calm situations, so it becomes second nature when needed.

_____

_____

_____

Stay neutral in heated moments, adopt the mirror technique. When interacting with an agitated player or coach, consciously mirror calm body language. Speak slowly and quietly, maintain a neutral facial expression, and keep your gestures minimal. This helps you stay composed and can also have a calming effect on others.

For recognizing and managing your emotional triggers, create an emotional inventory. After each game, jot down:

- Situations that triggered strong emotions
- How you reacted
- How you wish you had reacted

RULE 9.2

COMPOSURE TECHNIQUES—KEEPING YOUR COOL

Practice the techniques on the following pages to work on effective composure. Use the space provided to jot down your reflections and insights about your thoughts and experiences.

The neutral face technique. In front of a mirror, practice maintaining a neutral expression while imagining different scenarios that might trigger strong emotions during a game. This could be a disputed call, a confrontation with a coach, or a tense moment with a player. The goal is to develop a "poker face" that doesn't betray your emotions, even when feeling intense pressure.

Body language. Develop a calm posture routine that you can use during games. This might involve standing straight, relaxing your shoulders, and avoiding fidgeting or aggressive gestures. Practice this posture in low-stakes first, then gradually apply it in more intense games. For more ideas on this, refer to rule 6.2.

Use the breath-to-motion technique to channel emotions into focused energy. Whenever you feel emotional, take a deep breath through your nose and out through your mouth. As you exhale, focus on your next action—making a call, moving into position, or communicating with a player. This simple technique helps convert emotional energy into productive action.

RULE 9.3

PRESSURE AS OPPORTUNITY—TURNING STRESS INTO STRENGTH

Practice the techniques on the following pages to work on turning pressure into an opportunity. Use the space provided to jot down your reflections and insights about your thoughts and experiences.

Develop a pressure privilege phrase. This should be a short, powerful phrase reminding you of the honor of your role. It might be something like "I've earned this moment" or "This is why I officiate." Repeat this phrase to yourself during pre-game preparation and in high-pressure moments during the game.

Box breathing technique:

- Inhale quietly through your nose for 4 seconds
- Pause your breath for 4 seconds
- Exhale completely through your mouth for 4 seconds
- Pause your breath for 4 seconds

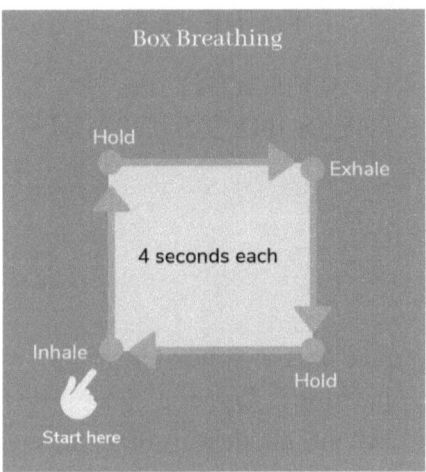

Practice this breathing pattern regularly to employ it during games and maintain composure easily. If you find that 4 seconds is too long and you get dizzy, try a shorter time frame. The key benefit of the strategy is steadying and making your breath consistent.

RULE 10

REFLECT AND GROW

"We do not learn from experience ... we learn from reflecting on experience."
—John Dewey

Rule 10.1: Systematic Self-Evaluation—The Path to Progress
Rule 10.2: Progress Tracking and Celebration—Measuring Success
Rule 10.3: Feedback and Sharing—Learning from Others

THIS MENTAL RULE EMPHASIZES THE POWER OF REFLECTION and self-improvement in officiating. By mastering the art of performance analysis and reflective practice, you enhance your ability to learn and grow from every experience, ensuring continuous improvement and increased effectiveness as an official.

This rule equips you with the tools to transform each game, regardless of its outcome, into a valuable learning opportunity, fostering ongoing development, and excellence in your officiating career.

RULE 10.1

SYSTEMATIC SELF-EVALUATION—THE PATH TO PROGRESS

PRACTICE THE TECHNIQUES ON THE FOLLOWING PAGES TO WORK on self-evaluation. Use the space provided to jot down your reflections and insights about your thoughts and experiences.

Create a post-game reflection routine. This should be a simple process you can complete within 15-30 minutes of every game you officiate. Here's a basic structure:

Quick debrief (5 minutes):
    Write down three things you did well
    Note 3 areas for improvement
    Record any unusual or challenging situations you encountered

Performance rating (2 minutes):
    Rate your overall performance on a scale of 1-10
    Briefly explain your rating

Key learnings (3 minutes):
    Write down the most important lesson from this game

Make this routine a non-negotiable part of your officiating practice. The goal is to capture your immediate thoughts and feelings while the game is still fresh in your mind.

Implement a game video review session within 48 hours of each game. If you don't have access to game film for every match, aim to review footage at least once a month. During this session:

Watch the full game or key segments
- Focus on your positioning, mechanics, and decision-making
- Compare your real-time decisions with what you see on film
- Note any discrepancies or insights

RULE 10.2

PROGRESS TRACKING AND CELEBRATION— MEASURING SUCCESS

Practice the techniques on the following pages to work on tracking your progress. Use the space provided to jot down your reflections and insights about your thoughts and experiences.

Create a progress journal. This should be a dedicated notebook or digital document where you record your performance insights after each game. Include:
- Areas for improvement: Note specific aspects of your officiating that need work.
- Progress tracking: Set specific, measurable goals for improvement and track your progress over time.
- Successes: Celebrate any achievements, no matter how small they seem.

    For example, after a game, you might write:
     - Area for improvement: Better positioning on corner kicks.
     - Progress: Successfully managed two corner kicks without issues.
     - Success: Handled a difficult coach interaction professionally.

Implement a celebration ritual. This could be as simple as treating yourself to a favorite meal after a game where you met one of your goals or sharing your successes with a colleague or mentor. The goal is to create a consistent way to acknowledge and celebrate your achievements.

Use a goal-setting template. At the start of each month or season, set three specific goals related to your officiating performance. These might include improving your reaction time, enhancing your communication with players, or refining your decision-making on particular types of calls. Track your progress towards these goals regularly, adjusting them as needed based on your reflections.

RULE 10.3

FEEDBACK AND SHARING—LEARNING FROM OTHERS

Practice the techniques on the following pages to work on developing effective feedback. Use the space provided to jot down your reflections and insights about your thoughts and experiences.

Adopt a feedback mindset. After each game, actively seek feedback from at least one source. This could be your officiating partners, a mentor or supervisor, or self-reflection through video review

When receiving feedback, practice the *Three A's*:
Acknowledge: Thank the person for their input
Ask: Seek clarification or examples if needed
Act: Determine one specific action you'll take based on the feedback if you agree

Implement or attend a group catch-up of trusted officials. Identify 2-3 trusted colleagues with whom you can regularly exchange experiences and insights. Set up a monthly call or meeting where each person shares:

- A challenge they faced and how they handled it
- A success story and what led to the positive outcome
- A question or area where they're seeking advice

Commit to a give-back goal to contribute to the broader officiating community. This could be:

- Volunteering to mentor a new official
- Offering to present at a local officiating clinic
- Writing an article for an officiating newsletter or website

Set a specific target, such as mentoring one new official per season or giving one presentation yearly.

RULE 11

STRENGTH IN NUMBERS

"Having fellow refs around you gives you great opportunities to develop. It will make you a better referee."
—*Carol Anne Chenard*

Rule 11.1: Building Relationships—The Power of Community
Rule 11.2: Mentorship and Learning—Passing on Wisdom
Rule 11.3: Community Support—Standing Together

THIS MENTAL RULE EMPHASIZES THE POWER OF COMMUNITY IN officiating. By mastering the art of building and leveraging referee networks, you enhance your resilience and access to knowledge, ensuring a more supported and successful officiating career. This rule equips you with the tools to build a strong support network, transforming your officiating journey from a solitary pursuit into a collective endeavor of growth and excellence.

RULE 11.1

BUILDING RELATIONSHIPS—THE POWER OF COMMUNITY

Practice the techniques on the following pages to work on your relationship and network building skills. Use the space provided to jot down your reflections and insights about your thoughts and experiences.

Create a connection calendar
Set a goal to make one meaningful connection within the officiating community each month. This could involve:
- Reaching out to a colleague you respect for a coffee or video chat
- Attending a local officiating meeting or workshop
- Participating in an online forum or social media group for officials

To make these interactions purposeful, prepare a few questions or topics you'd like to discuss. This preparation ensures that each connection is meaningful and contributes to your growth.

The three-tier networking strategy
-Local: Engage with officials in your immediate area or league
-Regional: Expand your network to include officials from neighboring areas or higher-level leagues
-National/international: Connect with officials from different parts of the country or world through online platforms or conferences
Set specific goals for each tier. For example, aim to know all of or most of the officials in your local league, attend one regional officiating event per year, and join an international officiating forum online.

Commit to a community contribution plan

The plan will lead you to participate more actively in officiating communities. Choose one way you can contribute your time or expertise each season. This might include:
- Volunteering to help organize a local officiating clinic
- Sharing your experiences or insights in an officiating newsletter or blog
- Offering to mentor a new official

RULE 11.2

MENTORSHIP AND LEARNING—PASSING ON WISDOM

Practice the techniques on the following pages to work on mentorship. Use the space provided to jot down your reflections and insights about your thoughts and experiences.

Create a mentorship framework.
This involves identifying two key roles:
Mentor: Find a veteran official who can guide you. Set up regular check-ins to discuss your progress, challenges, and goals.
Mentee: Offer to mentor a new official. Share your experiences, provide feedback, and help them set goals for improvement.

For example, you might meet with your mentor monthly to review your performance and discuss strategies for improvement. You might also set up bi-weekly calls with your mentee to review game footage and provide feedback on their officiating.

Implement the experience sharing cycle. Regularly share your experiences with fellow officials through informal discussions or more formal presentations at officiating clinics. This could involve:
- Discussing challenging situations and how you handled them
- Sharing tips for improving specific skills
- Reflecting on what you've learned from recent games or training sessions

Commit to a monthly share practice to make this sharing more systematic. Each month, write down one key lesson or insight you've gained from your officiating experiences. Share this with your mentor, mentee, or other officials through a newsletter or online forum.

RULE 11.3

COMMUNITY SUPPORT—STANDING TOGETHER

Practice the techniques on the following pages to work on community support skills. Use the space provided to jot down your reflections and insights about your thoughts and experiences.

Create a support network map. Identify at least three colleagues you can turn to for support or advice. This might include:

- A mentor or experienced official
- A peer who officiates at a similar level
- A colleague from a different officiating background or sport

Regularly check in with these individuals, offering support when needed and seeking advice when facing challenges.

Implement a community contribution plan. Commit to one specific way you'll contribute to the growth of the officiating community each season. This could be:

- Volunteering to help organize a local officiating clinic
- Writing an article for an officiating newsletter or blog
- Participating in a mentorship program for new officials

Set clear goals for your contribution and track your progress throughout the season.

Adopt the shared reflection practice. After each game or significant officiating event, take a few minutes to reflect on what you learned and how you can apply those lessons in the future. Share these reflections with your support network through a group chat, email, or in-person discussion.

RULE 12

THRIVING IN OFFICIATING

"It's what you learn after you think you know it all that really counts."
—*John Wooden*

Rule 12.1: Cultivating Curiosity—The Mind of a Learner
Rule 12.2: Practicing Gratitude—Finding Positivity
Rule 12.3: Continuous Learning and Growth—The Journey Never Ends
Bonus Rule: Holistic Well-being—Balancing Life and Sport

This mental rule emphasizes the importance of not just surviving, but thriving in officiating. Mastering these principles enhances your ability to find fulfillment, grow continuously, and maintain well-being, ensuring a long, successful, and satisfying career.

This rule equips you with the tools to transform the pressures of officiating into opportunities for personal and professional growth, allowing you to excel while maintaining a balanced and fulfilling life.

RULE 12.1

CULTIVATING CURIOSITY—THE MIND OF A LEARNER

Practice the techniques on the following pages to work on furthering your curiosity. Use the space provided to jot down your reflections and insights about your thoughts and experiences.

Create a curiosity journal. This should be a dedicated notebook or digital document where you regularly record questions, observations, and insights about officiating. Set aside some time after each game or training session to write down:
- One aspect of the game or rules that you want to explore further
- A situation that challenged your understanding or application of the rules
- An idea or approach you'd like to investigate

Review your journal weekly, choosing one topic to research more deeply.

The rule of the week practice. Each week, select one rule or aspect of officiating to study in depth. This might involve:
- Reading official interpretations and case studies
- Discussing the rule with colleagues or mentors
- Watching game footage to see how the rule is applied in various situations

Share your findings with fellow officials through informal discussions or by presenting at local officiating meetings.

Adopt the cross-sports approach. Regularly expose yourself to officiating practices from other sports or levels of play. This could involve:

- Attending a clinic or workshop for a different sport
- Shadowing an official in another league or level
- Reading officiating materials from various sports

RULE 12.2

PRACTICING GRATITUDE—FINDING POSITIVITY

Practice the techniques on the following pages to work on gratitude. Use the space provided to jot down your reflections and insights about your thoughts and experiences.

Create a pre-game gratitude ritual. Before each game, reflect on what you're thankful for. This might include:

- The opportunity to officiate
- The support of family or colleagues
- The chance to contribute to the sport

Write these reflections down in a gratitude journal, or take a moment to acknowledge them silently.

Implement the value in every assignment mindset. Regardless of the game's perceived importance, approach each assignment with purpose and enthusiasm. Remember that every game is an opportunity to improve, learn, and contribute to the sport.

RULE 12.3

CONTINUOUS LEARNING AND GROWTH—THE JOURNEY NEVER ENDS

Practice the techniques on the following pages to work on continuous learning. Use the space provided to jot down your reflections and insights about your thoughts and experiences.

Create a learning action plan. At the beginning of each season, set three specific learning goals:
- A technique you want to master or improve
- A concept from another sport you wish to explore and potentially adapt
- A rule or aspect of the game you want to investigate more deeply

Break each goal down into actionable steps and set deadlines for achieving them.

Implement the cross-sport study practice. Each month, choose an officiating technique or concept from a different sport to study. This might involve:

- Watching videos of officials in other sports
- Reading rulebooks or officiating manuals from different games
- Discussing techniques with officials from other sports

Reflect on how these insights might apply to your officiating and experiment with adapting them in your games.

BONUS RULE

HOLISTIC WELL-BEING—BALANCING LIFE AND SPORT

Practice the techniques on the following pages to work on your wellbeing. Use the space provided to jot down your reflections and insights about your thoughts and experiences.

Create a mindfulness routine. Before each game, take 5 minutes to center yourself:

- Find a quiet space and sit comfortably.
- Close your eyes and focus on your breath.
- Mentally scan your body, releasing any tension.
- Set an intention for the game (e.g., "I will officiate with clarity and fairness").

Practice this routine consistently to develop your ability to whistle with awareness.

Implement a post-game boundary routine. After each game:

- Take a few deep breaths
- Mentally "pack away" the game's events
- Change out of your officiating uniform
- Engage in a non-officiating activity you enjoy

This routine helps you leave the game on the field, separating your officiating role from your personal life.

Create a support network map.
Identify at least three sources of support:

- A trusted colleague or mentor in officiating
- A friend or family member outside of officiating
- A professional resource (e.g., counselor, sports psychologist)

Commit to seeking strength in support at least once a month or more frequently when facing challenges.

AFTERWORD
ELEVATING EXCELLENCE IN OFFICIATING

Congratulations on reaching the end of The Whistle Blower Workbook. By working through each section, you've gone far beyond simply reading rules: you've actively practiced, reflected, and applied powerful strategies to improve every aspect of your officiating life.

Reflecting on the journey, it's clear that excellence in officiating isn't confined to a single moment or skill. It comes from a balance of preparation, presence, communication, resilience, and a willingness to keep learning. Each rule in this workbook—whether about preparation, visualization, fitness, communication, emotional control, continuous learning, or community—forms part of a comprehensive system that supports you on and off the field.

Let's recap what you've strengthened by following the structure of the book:
· *Rules 1 to 3*: You've built a solid foundation, learning to prepare with intention, pay attention to details, harness visualization, and manage your energy: physical, mental, and emotional.
· *Rules 4 to 5*: You've developed adaptable mindsets, learning to focus, filter distractions, act with conviction, and accept what you can't control.
· *Rules 6 to 7*: Your skills in clear, confident, and flexible communication have improved, supported by positive self-talk and the power of ongoing self-reflection.
· *Rules 8 to 9*: You've discovered techniques for rapid mental and emotional recovery, built resilience, and learned to thrive under pressure.
· *Rules 10 to 12*: Most importantly, you've embraced growth, self-assessment, feedback, and the support of your officiating community, recognizing that the journey of continuous learning never ends.

Through the bonus rule, you're reminded to look after the whole self, balancing your love for officiating with life beyond the game.

Keep This Workbook Close

Use this workbook as a living guide: a place to revisit, update, and expand as you evolve. After each game, come back to these pages. Record what worked, what challenged you, and what you learned. Seek feedback, celebrate your progress, and set new goals aligned with the rules that matter most to your current stage.

Share and Grow Together

Growth thrives within a supportive community. Reach out to others—mentors, colleagues, and newcomers alike. Discuss your insights, offer encouragement, and learn from every experience together.

The Journey Continues

You are now equipped not just with rules, but with a practical, personal toolkit for lasting success. Let the principles, exercises, and reflections you've completed here reinforce your commitment to officiating and to life at your highest standard.

Blow the whistle with confidence, compassion, and curiosity. The rules in these pages are reminders: every day, every game, is another chance to put your best foot forward.

Shine Bright, Dr Jo

BONUS OFFER

WINNING AT WELLBEING: THE MENTAL FITNESS BLUEPRINT

Download your BONUS e-book of Winning at Wellbeing, a mental fitness blueprint for your officiating journey.

Scan the QR code or visit: https://books.drjolukins.com/tzgyllnm6p

ABOUT DR. JO

DR. JO IS OFTEN REFERRED TO AS THE PSYCHOLOGICAL INDIANA Jones of success! With over thirty years in the realm of sports psychology, she's on a quest to uncover the secrets behind peak performance.

She finds joy in running with friends (then drinking coffee with them), going on adventures with her husband and two sons, and reading and watching whatever sport she can! You can connect with Dr. Jo at www.drjolukins.com

A NOTE FROM DR. JO

If you enjoyed The Whistle Blower Workbook, I'd appreciate you sharing your views so others can benefit from your insights.

Leaving a review - whether on Amazon, Goodreads, your place of purchase, or your social media—helps more people discover the book and learn further in their officiating journey. I'd love to read your feedback! Please email me the link or a message to say hello at excel@drjolukins.com

Thank you for helping elevate the conversation in sport and performance,

Dr. Jo Lukins

STAY CONNECTED WITH DR. JO

Elevate your personal and professional game with The Locker Room's positive psychology insights. Dr. Jo presents offers avenues of connection through a weekly podcast

🎧 Tune into The Locker Room; and an insightful monthly newsletter 📖

Sign up for the newsletter & receive your *free* Confidence Checklist

The Locker Room Podcast

Confidence Checklist + Newsletter

READ MORE WITH DR. JO

The following books by Dr Jo are available at www.drjolukins.com or your favorite online or physical book store.

The Elite: Think like an Athlete, Succeed like a Champion, 2019

In the Grandstands: The Sporting Parents Guide to Raising a Confident & Happy Teens, 2020

The Game Plan: Your 5-month Coaching Program to Champion High-Performance Habits, 202

The Elite and The Game Plan 2-in-1 Book: Champion your Success with Elite Habits, 2023

Belief: Building Unshakeable Confidence, 2024

The Whistle Blower: The Mental Toughness Rulebook for Referees and Umpires, 2025

The Whistle Blower Workbook: The Mental Toughness Workbook for Referees and Umpires, 2025

www.ingramcontent.com/pod-product-compliance
Lightning Source LLC
Chambersburg PA
CBHW060358080526
44583CB00012B/379